EXPLORE
ANCIENT
EGYPT!

CARMELLA VAN VLEET
ILLUSTRATED BY ALEX KIM

Nomad Press

A division of Nomad Communications

10 9 8 7 6 5 4 3 2 1

ISBN: 978-0-9792268-3-0

Hieroglyphic alphabet on page 75 courtesy of
Colleen Manassa, Assistant Professor of Egyptology, Yale University.

Questions regarding the ordering of this book should be addressed to
Independent Publishers Group
814 N. Franklin St.
Chicago, IL 60610
www.ipgbook.com

Nomad Press
2456 Christian St.
White River Junction, VT 05001

green press
press
INITIATIVE

For Mom and Abbey, my bookends.

Other titles from Nomad Press

CONTENTS

LET'S EXPLORE EGYPT!

Y ou've probably played in sand or gone swimming. You've probably also played a board game or helped around the house. Maybe you've taken care of a pet or slept outdoors. Guess what? Kids who lived in ancient Egypt did these things, too!

Where was ancient Egypt? What was it like to live there? What did kids and their parents wear, eat, or do for work or fun? This book is going to explore ancient Egypt, an amazing place that existed thousands of years ago, from 3100 **BCE** to 639 **CE**!

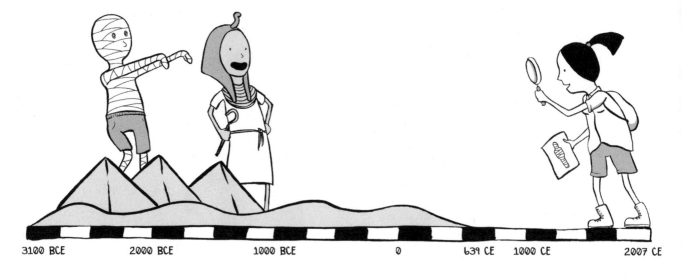

| 3100 BCE | 2000 BCE | 1000 BCE | 0 | 639 CE | 1000 CE | 2007 CE |

Explore Ancient Egypt! will answer many of your questions and share some really cool facts. You'll get to learn about things like **mummies**, **pyramids**, kohl makeup, and **pharaohs**. One of these famous pharaohs was King Tut. Did you know he's called the Boy King because he was just nine years old when he took over the throne?

Along the way, we're going to make lots of fun projects, play games, do activities, and hear some goofy jokes. Ready? Let's explore!

WHERE IN THE WORLD WAS ANCIENT EGYPT?

Ancient Egypt was in the northeastern part of Africa. It was in the **Sahara Desert**. The Sahara is the biggest and hottest desert in the world. A desert is an area with very little rain.

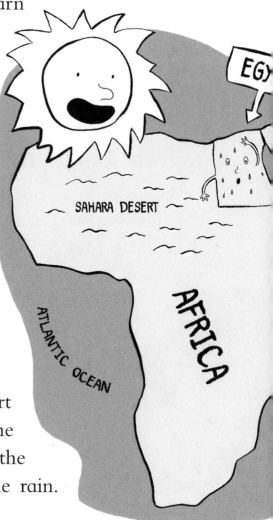

Ancient Egypt's daytime temperatures were over 100 degrees Fahrenheit. The heat and the sand made life tough for the ancient Egyptians. They had to be careful about sunburn, and sand got into everything. It even got into the bread they baked, which caused their teeth to wear down. Ouch!

But the desert also had its good points. For example, it protected ancient Egyptians from enemies. Not many people wanted to cross the hot, sandy land! And thanks to the desert, we know a lot about ancient Egypt. How? Well, the desert sand preserved a lot of ancient Egyptian buildings and things ancient people used. Since these things are still around, we can look at them and learn. Some people study buildings, art, and everyday objects from ancient Egyptian times. They are called **Egyptologists**.

Ancient Egypt was divided into two lands. One was Upper Egypt and the other was Lower Egypt. If you looked at a map of ancient Egypt, you'd see something strange. You might even say, "Hey, it's upside down!" That's because Upper Egypt was below Lower Egypt on the map. There is a simple reason for this. It has to do with the **Nile River**.

Words 2 Know

BCE: an abbreviation that means Before Common Era.

CE: an abbreviation that means Common Era, after the birth of Christ.

mummy: a dried and preserved dead body.

pyramid: large, stone structures with square bases and triangular sides where pharaohs were buried.

pharaoh: ancient Egyptian kings or rulers.

Sahara Desert: the largest, hottest desert in the world.

Egyptologist: someone who studies ancient Egypt.

3

INDIAN OCEAN

WOW

Nile Green is a color. It's a pale, yellowish-green. And, yep! It got its name from the color of the Nile River.

THE NILE RIVER

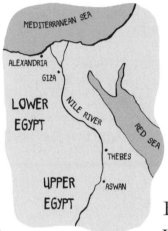

The Nile River is the longest river in the world. It's over 4,200 miles long and runs right through the Sahara Desert. It was very important to the ancient Egyptians. One of the neat things about the Nile is that it runs south to north. Most rivers run north to south. The land downstream was Lower Egypt. Because the other area was upstream, it was called Upper Egypt.

There is another neat thing about the Nile. It used to flood every year in ancient times. This flooding, called the **inundation**,

4

A SHIP FIT FOR A KING

Most of the small boats in ancient Egypt were made of reeds. To build bigger, wooden boats, the Egyptians had to get wood from different parts of the world. Wooden boats were often curved up at the ends just like the reed boats. These fancy, wooden boats were called **papyriform boats**. They were sometimes used as funeral boats to carry the pharaoh to his tomb.

One of the most famous papyriform boats is the **Royal Ship of Khufu.** Khufu was an Egyptian king. He was buried in the Great Pyramid. In 1954 Egyptologists found the ship buried near the Great Pyramid. The ship is 150 feet long and was in 1,200 pieces! They had to put it together like one big puzzle. Today it is inside a special museum that was built right over the spot where the pieces were found. We don't know if the ship was actually used as King Khufu's funeral boat. Maybe King Khufu just wanted a very fancy boat to use in the **afterlife**!

was the key to life in ancient Egypt. The floodwaters left behind **silt**. These silt deposits added minerals to the soil and made it rich and fertile. The ancient Egyptians planted crops in this soil.

Besides water and good soil for farmland, the Nile gave ancient Egyptians a place to swim and fish. It also gave them a way to travel. Ancient Egyptians were great boat builders. Poor people made small boats to use for fishing. These boats were made out of reeds. Guess what they were called? Reed boats!

Rich people had bigger boats made out of wood. They used these boats to travel up and down the Nile on vacation in style. Workers used even bigger boats, called barges, to move things like the rocks used to build pyramids and temples.

Ancient Egypt had two types of land areas. These two areas had colorful names. Ancient Egyptians called the land near the banks of the Nile the *Kemet*, which meant Black Land. This is because silt made the soil black. The ancient Egyptians called the desert *Deshret*, which meant the Red Land.

Words 2 Know

Nile River: the longest river in the world and an important part of ancient Egyptian life.

inundation: another word for flooding.

papyriform boats: wooden boats that curved up at the ends to look like reed boats, often used as funeral boats.

Royal Ship of Khufu: a famous example of a papyriform boat, found in pieces, buried near the Great Pyramid.

afterlife: the ancient Egyptians believed in life after death.

silt: the good farming soil left over after the Nile flooded.

5

MAKE A AND

Ancient Egyptians used symbols in their writing and art. The symbol for Lower Egypt was the papyrus plant. The symbol for Upper Egypt was the lotus flower. Many times, these two plants are shown together in ancient Egyptian art. This is done to represent how King Menes united the two lands around 3100 BCE.

1 To make a papyrus plant, use the green crayon to color both sides of a coffee filter. The filter is soft so be careful not to tear it while you color.

2 Fold the coffee filter in half. Fold it in half again. This is your plant bud.

3 Wrap one end of a pipe cleaner around the bottom, pointy end of the plant bud. The pipe cleaner is your plant's steam. Open up the other end of your coffee filter to finish your papyrus plant.

4 Roll some clay into a mound. Stick your plant's steam into the clay.

5 Make more papyrus plants and add them to the clay mound.

THEN & NOW

CAIRO

THEN: The capital of ancient Egypt was Memphis.

NOW: The capital of Egypt is Cairo.

PAPYRUS PLANT
A LOTUS FLOWER

1 To make a lotus flower, use the blue crayon to color both sides of a coffee filter. Fold the filter as you did before.

2 Carefully cut small triangles into the top edge of the filter. The lotus flower has pointy petals.

3 Wrap a green pipe cleaner around the bottom of the flower bud. Add the lotus flower to the mound of clay.

4 Egyptian artists often drew the lotus flower turned sideways. If you want, you can tilt your flower by bending the pipe cleaner.

Supplies

blue and green crayons
or colored pencils
coffee filters
green pipe cleaners
scissors
1 stick of clay

MAKE YOUR OWN

Reed boats were made out of the reeds of a papyrus plant. Because the reeds were bundled together, the ends of the boat curved up. Most ancient Egyptians used reed boats. Wooden boats were expensive. This is because there weren't many trees in the desert, and the trees that were there didn't make good planks. Wood had to come from other countries. Here's a way to make a model of a reed boat that really floats. You will be using spray paint for this project, so you'll need a grownup around.

1 Pinch one end of a straw and put it into the end of another straw. Make sure the bendable parts of the straws are at the outside ends. Do the same thing with the other straws. When you're done, you should have ten long straws.

2 Lay all the straws flat next to each other. Right now, your boat will look kind of like a raft.

3 Wrap a piece of duct tape around the middle.

4 At the flexible parts, bend the straws up. The boat will now be crescent-shaped. Pinch the ends of the straws together and tie them with a piece of string. Be sure to tie them tightly so the string doesn't slip off. Cut off any extra string.

5 Wrap a piece of duct tape around each bendy part of the straws. The tape will help your boat keep the right shape.

6 Follow the instructions on the spray paint can to paint your boat. Let it dry. Now, you're ready to put your reed boat in some water and watch it float!

Supplies

20 flexible drinking straws
duct tape
string or yarn
scissors
brown spray paint

REED BOAT

JUST FOR LAUGHS

Q: • What do you
• call a folder
where you
keep pictures of
Ancient Egypt?

A: A Nile file!

COOL ARTIFACT

The ancient Egyptians put a boat or a model of a boat into every tomb. This is because they believed the spirit needed a boat to travel into the afterlife.

PLAY AFTER A WHILE CROCODILE!

The Nile provided the ancient Egyptians with food and water, a place to play, and a way to travel. But, it could be a dangerous place, too. Many animals lived in or near the river. Ancient Egyptians always had to watch out for them. One of these dangerous animals was the crocodile. What would it be like to be constantly on guard? Play this game with some friends to get an idea.

1 Chose a player to be the crocodile. While the crocodile counts to 20, the other players spread out. Once they are away from the crocodile, they should pretend to do a common river activity. Here are some ideas: fish, swim, do laundry, paddle a boat.

2 While the other players are busy, the crocodile tries to sneak up and tag them.

3 If a player sees the crocodile, he or she can run away. The crocodile may chase the player.

4 To escape the crocodile, a player must stop pretending or running and yell, "After 'while, crocodile!" and sit down. If he or she can do this before being tagged, he or she is safe.

5 If the crocodile tags a player before he or she can say the phrase and sit down, the player is considered caught. He or she then becomes the new crocodile. The person who was the crocodile now pretends to visit the river. There is no winner in this game. Just keep playing until you and your friends get tired!

Supplies

3 or more players
a large area to run around in

EGYPTIAN HOMES

~~~~~~

Have you ever slept on the roof of your house? Ancient Egyptian families often did just that! Sometimes, they cooked on their roofs, too. They were able to do this because their roofs were flat.

But why would they do these things up on their roofs? Think about it. There was no electricity back then. No air conditioners or fans. Sleeping and cooking outdoors was a great way to keep cool. Of course, ancient Egyptians spent time inside their homes, too.

THEN & NOW

THEN: Most people lived along the Nile River.

NOW: Most of Egypt's population still lives right along the Nile River.

The average ancient Egyptian home had a simple, rectangular design and one or two bedrooms. It was about 350 to 400 square feet. This is roughly the same size as a two-car garage. Because wood was hard to find, ancient Egyptians used **mudbricks** to build their houses. To make a mudbrick, a builder mixed **clay** from the banks of the Nile with straw and pebbles and water. Then the mixture would be poured into molds and left to dry in the sun. After a few days the mudbricks were ready to use, to build a house. Ancient Egyptians painted their houses white. The white helped reflect the sun's light and keep the houses cool. To keep the sun (and bugs) out, ancient Egyptians hung woven mats over their windows.

The homes of wealthy Egyptians were bigger and nicer than the homes of common folks. The rich could afford houses that were two or three stories high. Their homes also had beautiful gardens and pools for

12

Words 2 Know

mudbricks: bricks made of a mix of clay, pebbles, straw, and water and dried in the sun.

clay: a material found in nature that is sticky and easily molded when wet and hard when baked or dried.

decoration. There was room for servants and space for a business. While most ancient Egyptians went to the bathroom outside, the wealthy had toilets. These ancient toilets were wooden benches with a hole in the middle and a bowl underneath the hole.

FURNITURE

Inside, ancient Egyptian homes were colorful. People painted their walls with designs or scenes from nature. The walls also had special shelves for statues of household gods. Floors were usually bare earth. The wealthy had tiled floors, though.

Ancient Egyptians had very little furniture. This was true even for the rich. Some people used beds made out of simple, wood frames with leather or wood slats. Others used mattresses stuffed with straw. But most people just slept on mats on the floor. Does that sound uncomfortable? Here's something else that might sound uncomfortable. Instead of pillows, ancient Egyptians rested their heads on hard, crescent-shaped stands!

13

COOL ARTIFACT

We don't know why, but some ancient Egyptian beds were tilted. A footboard kept a sleeper from sliding off his or her bed.

WOW

Like us, ancient Egyptians had pets. They kept animals like birds and monkeys. But the most popular pets were cats and dogs.

Most ancient Egyptians sat on mats or on short stools that they carried from room to room. They stored their food, clothes, makeup, and other belongings in baskets. They also stored things in wooden boxes. Homes usually had a table and an oil lamp, too.

CHAIRS

Most ancient Egyptians didn't have chairs. If a family did have a chair, it was saved for guests or the head of the household. Ancient Egyptian chairs were different from the chairs we have in two ways. First, their legs were shorter. This was probably because ancient Egyptians were shorter than the average person today.

The second unusual thing was that the chair legs were often carved to look like animal legs! Lion paws, crocodile feet, or gazelle legs were popular choices. Along with fancy legs, ancient Egyptian chairs also had beautiful decorations. This was especially true if the chair belonged to a rich family. Paintings or carvings of birds or lotus flowers were common. Sometimes, the name of the person who owned the chair was carved into it. These fancy chairs were made out of wood, animal skin, or even solid silver or gold. Many of them just had backs with no armrests. Chairs with armrests were only for the really rich or powerful, like a pharaoh.

HOUSEHOLD GODS

Ancient Egyptians believed in many gods. Each **god** had a special power or job. Many ancient Egyptians kept small statues of gods in their homes. Two of the most popular household gods were **Taweret** and **Bes**.

Taweret was the **goddess** who protected mothers and children. She had the head and body of a pregant hippo, the back of a crocodile, and the paws of a lion. Ancient Egyptians made her look this way because they knew lions, hippos, and crocodiles are protective of their young. They wanted Taweret to have the same quality.

Bes was a strange-looking god. He had the body of a dwarf, big animal ears, and a lion's face. He is often shown sticking out his tongue! Bes was the god of fun and games.

Taweret

Words 2 Know

god: a being believed to have special, superhuman powers.

Taweret: the ancient Egyptian household goddess who protected mothers and children.

Bes: the ancient Egyptian household god of fun and games.

goddess: a female god.

WOW

Cats were worshipped in ancient Egypt. They were allowed to sit under chairs. Artists made statues of them. At one point in history, you could be punished by death just for hurting a cat. Dogs were highly valued, too. Ancient Egyptians considered dogs to be a family member. How do we know this? Because they gave their dogs names, and ancient Egyptians believed names had magical powers. Pet cats weren't usually given names.

WHAT'S A SOUL HOUSE?

The ancient Egyptians believed a person had many parts. One part was your body. One part was your name. Your **Ba** was your personality. Your **Ka** was your spirit twin. Your **Akh** was created after your Ka and Ba got together in the afterlife. And your **Shadow** protected all the other parts.

Ancient Egyptians believed the Ka needed a place to live after a person died. So what did they do? They built small, model houses for the Ka. These models were called Soul Houses. Soul Houses were usually made out of clay. Inside were clay versions of food, furniture, tools, clothes, and everything a person might need in the afterlife. Ancient Egyptians believed models of things could magically become real in the afterlife. Soul Houses were buried along with the person who died.

16

OTHER IMPORTANT ANCIENT EGYPTIAN GODS

Ra: the sun god.

Osiris: god of the afterlife.

Isis: goddess of motherhood and wifehood. She was married to Osiris.

Horus: the son of Osiris and Isis.

Ma'at: the goddess of order and truth.

Atum: the creator god.

Hapy: the Nile god.

Ra   Isis   Horus

HOT AND COOL COLORS!

The ancient Egyptians painted their houses white and wore light-colored clothes to keep cool. In this experiment, you can see for yourself if white really does keep things cooler and if black really does heat things up. You'll need a warm, sunny day for this project.

1 Place an ice cube in each dish. Carry the dishes and paper outside. Find a sunny spot to set up your experiment.

2 Place one of the dishes in the middle of the white piece of paper. Place the other dish in the middle of the black piece of paper.

3 Observe what happens to the ice for the next hour. You don't have to stay outside the whole time. You can go inside and check on your experiment every 15 minutes if you'd like.

Things to think about

👁 Which ice cube melted the fastest?

👁 Did it melt a little faster or a lot faster?

👁 The color white reflects the sun's rays and therefore keeps things cooler. Did your experiment prove or disprove this?

👁 Feel the corners of the pieces of paper. Which one feels warmer? Why do you think this is?

Supplies

2 ice cubes, both the same size

2 shallow dishes, both exactly the same

1 piece of white construction paper

1 piece of black construction paper

MAKE AN

Egyptian headrests were made of many kinds of material. Most were carved out of wood. Pharaohs' headrests were often made of ivory or gold. The directions for this project call for gold spray paint, but you can decorate your headrest any way you'd like. You'll be using wire cutters and spray paint for this project so have a grownup nearby. This project is messy. Put plenty of newspaper on your work area.

1 You'll need two full-size sheets of newspaper for this step. First, fold the sheets lengthwise. Next, fold the sheets in half widthwise and then in half again. Keep folding until you have a strip that is about 3 inches wide and 12 inches long.

2 Roll the strip up into a tight, 3-inch-high newspaper log. Use some tape to keep the newspaper from unrolling.

3 Stand the newspaper log up on the middle of the craft board. Tape it to the board. This will be the stand for your headrest.

4 Cut your piece of wire. Be careful! The ends of the wire might be sharp. Bend the wire

Supplies

newspaper
masking tape
piece of wooden craft board, 5 inches by 7 inches
wire cutters
8-inch piece of a wire hanger
2 cups flour
1 cup of water
bowl
gold spray paint

into a crescent so that the ends line up with the ends of the craft board.

5 Wrap several pieces of newspaper around the wire. Secure the newspaper with tape. This piece is your headrest. Tape the headrest to the top of the stand.

EGYPTIAN HEADREST

6 Mix the flour and water in a bowl to make papier-mâché. If you run out of papier-mâché later on, you can make more by mixing two parts flour to one part water.

7 Tear several sheets of newspaper into strips. Dip the paper strips into the flour mixture.

8 Cover your stand and headrest with strips of papier-mâché. You'll need several layers to make your headrest strong. When you're done, let the project dry completely.

9 Finally, paint your headrest. When the paint is dry, you can try out your headrest! Do you think it will be more comfortable than your pillow?

MAKE A STOOL

The legs of ancient Egyptian chairs and stools were often carved to look like animal legs. Because they had only a few of them, or maybe even just one, ancient Egyptians carried their stools from room to room. Here's a fun way to make your own short stool with animal legs. You'll need an adult's help with the hot glue gun.

1 Use the craft glue to glue the pieces of cardboard together, one right on top of the other. This will be your seat. Let the glue dry while you move on to the next step.

2 Cover the outside of each soup can with a piece of the brown bag. Glue the paper to the can with the craft glue. One way to measure the right length is to lay the can down and roll it up in the paper. Then just cut off any extra.

3 The covered cans will be your stool legs. Decorate the cans to look like animal legs or paws.

4 Have an adult help you glue the soup cans to the bottom of the cardboard seat with the hot glue gun. Put one can in each corner, not too close to the edge. When the glue is dry, have a seat and relax, ancient Egyptian style!

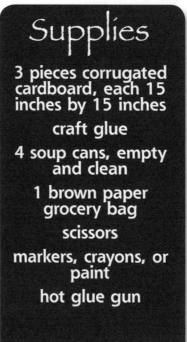

Supplies

3 pieces corrugated cardboard, each 15 inches by 15 inches

craft glue

4 soup cans, empty and clean

1 brown paper grocery bag

scissors

markers, crayons, or paint

hot glue gun

BEER, BREAD & BARTERING

Ancient Egyptians had many different jobs. Some were artists. Some were craftspeople or pyramid builders. Others were **scribes** or important government workers. But most ancient Egyptians were farmers.

They farmed the rich soil left behind by the Nile floodwaters. Even though farmers had the important job of feeding everyone, they had a low social status. This means that farmers were poor and they weren't highly respected.

THE SEASONS

In ancient Egypt the year was divided into three seasons. The first one was Akhet. This season lasted from June to September. During this season, the Nile flooded and its water covered the farmlands. Many farmers spent this time helping to build temples and pyramids. The second season was Peret. It went from October to February. This was the growing season when crops were planted. The last season was Shemu. It was from March to May. During this time, crops were **harvested**.

22

AKHET   PERET   SHEMU

Ancient Egyptian farmers planted lots of different crops. Vegetables like onions, lettuce, lentils, peas, and cucumbers were popular. Farmers also grew fruit. Many of the fruits around in ancient Egypt are ones we eat today, like apples and grapes. Dates, figs, and pomegranates were other fruits common in ancient Egypt. Spices and herbs such as cumin, mustard, cinnamon, dill, and coriander were important to the ancient Egyptians. Spices were used to add flavor to foods, treat illnesses, and even to make a mummy!

Besides fruits and vegetables, ancient Egyptians ate fish. That's not surprising since they lived near a river! They also kept goats and geese for milk and eggs. There were wild animals for meat, but most people didn't eat meat. Meat was saved for special occasions like feasts or weddings. These events were big affairs with lots of food, and music and dancers for entertainment. Musicians played instruments such as the drum or harp.

FAVORITE FOODS

No matter who you were in ancient Egypt—rich or poor, grownup or child—you ate bread and drank beer! Bread and beer were the "staples," or main foods, of the ancient Egyptians. Bread was made out of emmer wheat, and sometimes workers were paid with emmer wheat or beer.

It might seem strange to us that everyone drank beer, but it wasn't strange to the ancient Egyptians. Their beer was different from the beer we have today. Ancient Egyptian beer was made from leftover bread dough. Beer makers wet down the dough and turned it into **mash**. Then, the mash was left to **ferment**. Ancient Egyptian beer was probably sweet tasting and thick. Because it was made of bread, it was nutritious. It was more like a food than a drink.

Bread makers made all kinds of different bread. Some were sweet. Others were bland. Some were light and airy. Others were flat. Bread came in many different shapes, too: round, oval, or cone. Sometimes, loaves of bread were even formed into animal shapes. Bread makers

23

scribe: a person who read and wrote hieroglyphs, the ancient Egyptian writing.

harvest: to pick or pull crops out of the ground when they are ripe.

mash: grain soaked in hot water to be used in making alcohol.

ferment: a chemical breaking down of a substance caused by an enzyme.

cooked their bread in short, dome-shaped ovens made out of clay. One bad thing about baking bread in the desert was the sand. Sand got into the dough and baked into breads. When ancient Egyptians ate the bread, the sand wore down their teeth. This caused terrible and painful infections and rotten teeth. Some experts believe that these infections might have been bad enough to kill some people.

BARTERING

Ancient Egyptians didn't have grocery stores. The bought their goods at open markets. An open market is a place where sellers set up tents or tables to sell their products. The ancient Egyptians also did not use money. They used something called a **bartering** system.

A bartering system is where people trade one thing for another. For example, pretend you wanted a bookmark your friend made. You might trade a bracelet you made for the bookmark. That's bartering.

But what if the bracelet you made had lots of beads and took you a really long time to make? What if it was more valuable than the bookmark? The same thing happened in ancient Egypt.

SHADUFS

The floodwaters of the Nile gave the ancient Egyptians rich soil to farm. Silt from the flooding water stayed behind and made the soil rich and fertile. It was just like fertilizer being brought in each year. But remember, the ancient Egyptians lived in a desert. There was very little rain. So how did they water their crops? They dug out ditches and filled them with water. These ditches ran through the farmland. But, wait a minute, you might be thinking. How did they get the water into the canals in the first place? Good question. The answer is, they used a **shaduf**.

A shaduf is a simple device that uses a bucket on one end of a long pole with a counterweight on the other end. The pole rests on a stand. The whole thing kind of looks like a giant seesaw. A farmer would lower the bucket into the water and fill it up. Then, the heavy weight at the other end would help lift the water bucket up. After the water was lifted up, it could be poured into the canals. Shadufs were such a great invention that they are still used in Egypt and other parts of the world.

25

COOL ARTIFACT

Ancient Egyptians didn't use forks, knives, and spoons. They used their fingers to eat and then cleaned their hands in small bowls of water.

THEN & NOW

THEN: Ancient Egyptians bartered for goods they needed.

NOW: Egyptians still have open street markets, called souks, but they don't barter. They use paper money called an Egyptian pound and coins called piastres.

26

Sometimes, one thing was more valuable than another. To keep things fair, the ancient Egyptians used a special weight, called a *deben,* to measure things. Sellers would place a deben (or several of them) on one side of a scale and place the item to be sold on the other side of the scale. Then, they could decide how much the item could be traded for. For example, one *deben* of emmer wheat (which was valuable) might have been traded for three *debens* of onions (which were less valuable).

MEDICINE IN ANCIENT EGYPT

Besides tooth infections caused by sand in their bread, ancient Egyptians suffered from other illnesses and injuries. Many of these ailments are the same that we have today. For example, ancient Egyptians had colds, stomachaches, sore throats, and broken bones.

They also had more serious illnesses like cancer or the bubonic plague. But ancient Egyptians didn't know about germs or viruses. They thought evil spirits caused people to get sick. They treated illnesses with spells. A **spell** is a word or group of words that is thought to have magic powers to heal a person.

These spells were performed by a **priest**. Ancient Egyptian priests weren't really spiritual leaders. They were more like helpers.

Many times, ancient Egyptian priests also treated illnesses with natural cures. These cures included eating or drinking special things. For example, an ill person might be told to eat garlic, onions, or certain spices, or to drink castor oil. Honey was another popular, natural cure. Today, we know that some of these foods, like garlic and honey, can kill bad germs and really help someone who is sick!

JUST FOR LAUGHS

Brother: Would you like some Egyptian sweet bread?

Sister: What's Egyptian sweet bread?

Brother: You know, the kind of cake mummy used to make.

Words2Know

27

bartering: a system where people trade one thing for another.

shaduf: a simple device that uses a bucket and a counterweight on a long pole to lift water out of one place and move it to another.

spell: a word or group of words that the ancient Egyptians believed had magical powers to heal.

priest: a person who helped take care of sick people and took care of and ran the temples in ancient Egypt.

MAKE DRIED APPLES

The ancient Egyptians didn't have refrigerators to keep foods fresh. To preserve foods, they dried them in the sun. You need several hot, sunny days with low humidity to dry fruit. This kind of weather is easy to find in the Sahara Desert. It's not so easy to find many other places! Here's a great way to make dried apples at home. You'll be using an oven and a knife, so ask a grownup to help. Also, since you'll be working with food for this activity, make sure you wash your hands before you begin.

1 First, peel the skin off of the apples and take out the cores. Cut the apples into rings that are about a quarter-inch thick. Rings work the best.

2 Dip your apple rings into the lemon juice. The lemon juice will help keep the apples from turning brown. If you don't have lemon juice, you can use pineapple or orange juice.

3 Put a piece of parchment paper on your baking sheet. Lay the apple rings on the baking sheet.

Make sure they aren't touching each other.

4 Next, put your fruit in the oven to dry. It will take several hours. You'll know they are done when the rings are soft and chewy. Have a grownup help you check on them since the oven may be hot.

5 Let the apple rings cool. Now you have a healthy snack you can take anywhere! Store the leftovers in a sealed baggie or container. They will keep for a couple of weeks.

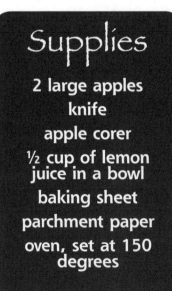

Supplies

2 large apples
knife
apple corer
½ cup of lemon juice in a bowl
baking sheet
parchment paper
oven, set at 150 degrees

ANIMAL-SHAPED BREAD

You'll be working with food for this activity. Make sure you wash your hands before you begin and ask a grown-up for help.

1 Put the yeast and the warm water in the bowl. Use the spoon to stir the mixture until the yeast is completely dissolved.

2 Add the honey and salt. Stir until the honey and salt dissolve.

3 Add 1 cup of flour. Now comes the fun, messy part! Use your hands to mix the flour into the liquid. Keep adding a little flour at a time, until the dough is soft.

4 Mix the dough with your hands for about five minutes. This is called kneading. The dough shouldn't stick to your hands. If it does, add more flour. If it's too dry and doesn't hold together, add a few drops of water.

5 Next, put the dough ball on a lightly floured surface and use it to make an animal-shaped loaf of bread! You can make any kind of animal you want, but common animals in ancient Egypt were cats, dogs, monkeys, and snakes.

6 When you're happy with the shape, lay the dough animal on the baking sheet.

7 Bake your bread animal for about 10 to 15 minutes. When it's golden brown, take it out, let it cool, and then enjoy!

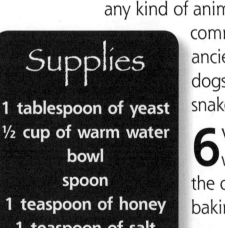

Supplies

1 tablespoon of yeast
½ cup of warm water
bowl
spoon
1 teaspoon of honey
1 teaspoon of salt
1 cup plus ½ cup of flour
baking sheet, lightly greased
oven set at 400 degrees

HOST A BARTERING DAY

The more people you have to do this activity, the more fun it will be. Ask your teacher if you can do this activity with your classmates, or invite the neighborhood gang over. Each person will each need one dozen, handmade items. Some ideas: bookmarks, bracelets, picture frames, clay animals, and paper airplanes. These items will be your products.

1 First you need to set up. You should each lay your items out on a towel or table. You'll want to make your display look good so people will want your product. Decorate your area with a colorful sign, balloons, or in some other way.

Supplies

plenty of friends

large area to move around in

beach towels or small tables

handmade products

decorations like balloons or a sign

lunch bags or plastic baggies

2 After everyone is done setting up, the entire group should spend fifteen minutes walking around, looking at each other's products. This is the time for everyone to think about what they'd like to barter for.

3 For the next step, you'll need to divide the group into four equal sizes. Decide which group is going first. Group #1 should put some of their products into their bags. Next, they can wander around the open market, making trades. Players can go back to their displays if they need more items to bargain with. For the moment, Group #1's displays will have no seller. If someone wants to make a trade for one of their products, he or she can come back later or make the trade with the seller while walking around.

4 Next, Group #2 gets a turn to trade. Then, it's Group #3's turn. Group #4 goes last.

5 Some items may be things that a lot of people want. The seller may price her product higher by asking for several, different items. You might have to make lots of trades in order to get something you really want!

6 After each group has had a turn, the whole group can spend ten minutes making any last-minute trades with anyone they missed. Now you've shopped ancient-Egypt style!

WRITE A HOME

We know a lot about how the ancient Egyptians handled illnesses because they wrote instructions and spells down. What would you tell someone about how to cure a certain illness or aches and pains at home? For example, do you know a sure way to stop pesky hiccups? Here's a fun way to create your own home-remedy book. Remember: a home remedy is something you can do at home, without going to the doctor or the store for medicine. Of course, if you're really sick or in a lot of pain you should definitely go see a doctor!

Supplies
notebook paper
pen or pencil
clipboard
notecards (any size)
hole punch
notebook ring

REMEDY BOOK

1 Spend some time thinking about any home cures or remedies you know. For example, maybe holding your breath and counting to ten always cures your hiccups. Maybe standing on your head and singing the alphabet does the trick instead. Do you know any ways to cure warts, headaches, toothaches, stomachaches, or a stuffy nose? How about special ways to take out a splinter? Or make a sunburn or bug bite feel better? Or get gum out of your hair? Write your ideas down on notebook paper. Use your imagination!

2 Interview your friends and family. Ask them if they know any home remedies. Their remedies can be for something on your list or for something new. Use the clipboard and more notebook paper to write their ideas down, too.

3 Organize all the remedies. You can put all the hiccup cures in one pile, all the stomach cures in another pile, remedies for skin problems in another, and so on.

4 Once you have the remedies in groups, copy them onto the notecards. Punch a hole in the top left corner of each card.

5 Open the notebook ring and put all the notecards on it. Now you've got your very own home-remedies book! You can even make copies of your book and share them with other people. It would make an interesting gift!

for hiccups:
1. jump up and down.
2. hold breath.

PLAYTIME

Most kids in ancient Egypt had chores. They had to help around the house or with the family business. If their families were farmers, children had to help plant and harvest crops.

Of course, kids had plenty of time for fun, too. They played board games, danced, wrestled, played Leap Frog and Tug-a-War, swam, and had races. Does this sound like anyone you know?

Ancient Egyptian kids played with all kinds of toys, too. For example, marbles were popular. They were made out of smooth stones. Playing catch was also popular. There was no rubber in ancient Egypt, so kids made balls by rolling and wrapping pieces of rags. Girls often played with dolls made out of rags or paddles.

Archaeologists are people who study ancient cultures by looking at **artifacts**. Artifacts are simple objects from a culture or time period, like toys. Archaeologists studying ancient Egypt have found animal pull toys. These animal pull toys look a lot like the pull toys you might have played with when you were a toddler. Kids or parents made most of the toys in ancient Egypt, because there weren't any toy stores.

35

MUSIC

From paintings inside tombs and on pottery, we know music was very important to ancient Egyptians. Children learned to play instruments from their parents or other instructors. There were professional musicians, whose job it was to play at religious ceremonies or to entertain at parties. There were also professional dancers and singers, because where there's music, there is singing and dancing, right?! We know some **lyrics** to ancient Egyptian songs because they were written on tomb walls.

DID YOU KNOW?

We don't know what the real rules for Senet were. The ancient Egyptians didn't write any down, or if they did, we haven't found them yet. But whatever the rules were, you can bet kids tried their best to follow them. Cheating was a big no-no in ancient Egypt. A cheater could be kicked or hit with sticks! A couple of people have come up with modern rules for Senet, based on what they think the rules might have been.

Besides playing with toys, ancient Egyptians played board games. Kings, queens, rich, poor, grownups, and children—it didn't matter! Everyone loved board games. There were many of them. Hounds and Jackals was kind of like the board game Chutes and Ladders. Mancala was a strategy game that used stones and bowls or shallow holes in the ground. Mancala is a great game that is still around. Maybe you've played it.

The most popular board game of all was called Senet. In this game two players take turns moving their pieces around a board. The winner is the person who gets all of his or her pieces off the board first. It's a little like our game Backgammon. Some people believe Senet might have had special, religious meaning. They believe this because Senet games were often played inside tombs.

Ancient Egyptians played many kinds of musical instruments. And many of these instruments are familiar to us today. They had flutes, trumpets, lyres, lutes, harps, bells, oboes, and rattles. They also played drums and even had an instrument that was like a guitar. Even though their instruments were similar to ones we have, we don't know how ancient Egyptian music really sounded. This is because we don't know how to read their music. Were notes played quickly or slowly? Were they long or short? Were they loud or soft? What do *you* think?

archaeologist: someone who studies ancient cultures by looking at artifacts.

artifact: a simple object like a tool from a culture or time period.

lyrics: words to songs.

SCHOOL IN ANCIENT EGYPT

Most ancient Egyptian children did not go to school. They learned the family trade from their parents. A trade is a job or business. For example, an ancient Egyptian boy might have learned to be a farmer or pottery maker from his father. An ancient Egyptian girl might have learned to be a bread maker from her mother. A few boys and girls learned to read a little, but there were no textbooks.

37

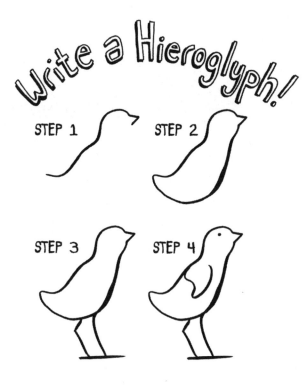

Write a Hieroglyph!

STEP 1

STEP 2

STEP 3

STEP 4

38

Instead, kids learned from a book called *The Book of Instruction*. It was a collection of advice on how to do well in life and be a good person.

A few children learned outside of the home. Some of them were **apprentices**. An apprentice is someone who learns to do a job by working for someone in that job. The only children who went to a formal school were those learning to be **scribes**. A scribe is a person who read and wrote **hieroglyphs**, the ancient Egyptian writing. Being a scribe was a very important job. They were in charge of recording all kinds of business and government deals. They were also in charge of decorating the walls of tombs and pyramids. Scribes usually came from wealthy families.

THE ROYAL LIBRARY OF ALEXANDRIA

Alexandria was a city in ancient Egypt. It was a great place of learning where many of the world's great thinkers visited. These great thinkers gathered to talk to one another and learn or teach about the latest discoveries in math or science. Alexandria had an amazing library called the **Royal Library of Alexandria**. It was built around 288 BCE and had over 500,000 books and scrolls. **Scrolls** were pieces of papyrus glued together and then rolled up. They were rolled-up books! Because it had so many books and great thinkers who visited, the Royal Library of Alexandria was like the world's first university!

The library existed for about 200 years until it was destroyed by a series of fires.

They started their education at around age ten. Scribes didn't use paper and pencils like students use today. And they didn't have desks. They sat cross-legged on the floor. They practiced writing on pieces of thin stone or pottery called **ostraca**.

This is because **papyrus**, the paper Egyptians made out of the papyrus plant, was too expensive for practicing. Instead of a pencil, young scribes used reeds and ink. A scribe would chew the end of a reed to make it into a brush. There were so many hieroglyphs to learn that it could take as long as ten years to become a scribe.

Words 2 Know

apprentice: someone who learns to do a job by working for someone who already does the job.

scribe: a person who read and wrote hieroglyphs, the ancient Egyptian writing.

hieroglyphs: the symbols that made up the written language of ancient Egypt.

ostraca: pieces of pottery used to practice writing.

papyrus: paper made from the papyrus plant and used by the ancient Egyptians.

Royal Library of Alexandria: a great library in Alexandria, Egypt, that had half a million books and scrolls.

scroll: pieces of papyrus glued together and then rolled up.

39

COOL ARTIFACT

King Tut's tomb had four sets of Senet. The largest one was as big as a small table. It was made of gold, ebony, and ivory and had King Tut's name engraved on it. It was truly a game fit for a king!

MAKE A RAG BALL

Children love balls and play lots of games using them, but you've probably never made your own before!

1 Tear two-thirds of the sheet into strips 2 to 3 inches wide and 1 to 2 feet long. If you don't have an old sheet, you can use old T-shirts. Lightweight material works the best. You might need to use scissors to get the strips started.

2 Scrunch up the remaining one-third of the sheet into a ball. This will be your ball's center. Tie several torn strips around the center ball to hold it together.

3 Now wrap strips of material around the ball's center. You don't need to tie these strips. Keep wrapping the strips around the ball in a crisscross fashion. Make sure to wrap the strips as tightly as you can. Tuck the ends of strips under other strips as you go.

4 When your ball is almost as big as you want it to be, start tying (instead of just wrapping) the strips again. Your knots don't have to be big, but they should be tight.

Supplies

old bed sheet
scissors
newspaper
craft glue
fabric paint, any color or colors

5 When the ball is the size you want, tuck in the knots and ends wherever you can. This will help make the outside of your ball smooth.

6 Cover your work surface with newspaper. Use a little bit of the glue to glue down the edges of the top strips. This will help keep your ball from unraveling when you play with it. Let the glue dry.

7 Use the fabric paint to paint the ball. Ancient Egyptian children painted their balls bright colors, but you can use any color or design you'd like. When the paint is dry, your ancient Egyptian–style ball is ready to throw and catch! Remember: even though it's made out of soft material, your rag ball will still be pretty hard. Be careful not to hit anyone or anything breakable with it.

THEN & NOW

THEN: There were no formal schools.

NOW: There are around 15,000 elementary schools in Egypt.

MAKE YOUR OWN

This board game is called Work or Play. It's not a real game that ancient Egyptian children played, but it is a fun way to learn about their chores!

1 Use the ruler and a marker to draw 15 squares on the poster board. The squares need to be touching each other. They can be in a straight line or a line that bends, or you can make up your own path! You'll need space to write in each square, so don't make them too small. Now label each square.

- In the first square, write: *BREAKFAST TIME*

- In the second square, write: *Help clean breakfast dishes. Move ahead two spaces.*

- In the third square, write: *Go to scribe school. Move ahead three spaces.*

- In the fourth square, write: *Feed the family dog.*

- In the fifth square, write: *Forget to sweep. Lose one turn.*

- In the sixth square, write: *Help plant onions.*

- In the seventh square, write: *Help Mom bake bread. Move ahead two spaces.*

- In the eighth square, write: *Work as an apprentice. Roll again.*

BOARD GAME

- In the ninth square, write: *Watch little brother. Move ahead one space.*
- In the tenth square, write: *Help with the harvest. Move ahead two spaces.*
- In the eleventh square, write: *Practice reading from the Book of Instruction.*
- In the twelfth square, write: *Fold clothes.*
- In the thirteenth square, write: *Carry storage baskets to the roof. Roll again.*
- In the fourteenth square, write: *Break a pot while playing catch. Move back three spaces.*
- In the last square, write: *PLAYTIME!*

2 After you fill in the squares, you can decorate the rest of your game board if you'd like. You can draw hieroglyphs or pictures of children doing the chores that are listed on the board.

To play

1 Each player places a token on BREAKFAST TIME (square #1). Players take turns rolling the dice. The highest roller is the player to go first in the game.

2 Player #1 rolls one die and moves the correct number of spaces. Once there, he or she follows the instructions to move forward or back, lose a turn, or roll again. Then, he or she waits for his next turn. If there are no instructions to move, the player remains on the square until his or her next turn.

3 Players take turns rolling the die, moving, and following the instructions. To win, a player must roll the die so that he or she lands directly on PLAYTIME!

43

PLAY TUG-A-WAR

Ancient Egyptian children played several games that are still around today. For example, they played Leap Frog. They also played a variation of Leap Frog called *khuzza lawizza*. In this game, two players sat on the ground facing each other and holding hands. Other players would try to jump over their hands. For each round, the kids' raised their hands higher. Tug-a-War is another game ancient Egyptian children played. Here's a fun variation.

1 Use the chalk to draw a straight line on the sidewalk. If you don't have a piece of chalk or want to play this game inside, just find a line on the floor. For example, you might be able to find a line in your kitchen floor design. You can also make a line by laying out a jump rope or a piece of tape. This would work on the grass, too.

2 Players stand on the line, about three feet apart. The players can be facing each other or opposite directions.

3 Next, roll the towel lengthwise. Each player takes an end of the towel and holds it in the hand that is closest to their opponent. You can hold the towel with both hands or keep one hand free to help you balance.

4 On the count of three, each player begins pulling the towel. The winner is the one who knocks the other player off balance and causes him or her to step off the line.

Supplies

chalk or tape or piece of rope

two players

towel

MAKING OSTRACA

Ancient Egyptian children who were learning to be scribes practiced writing on ostraca. Ostraca were thin pieces of pottery or stone. Here's an easy way to make something similar to ostraca. Since you'll be using spray paint, be sure to have a grownup help you.

1 Lay your plant saucer upside down on the newspaper. The bottom of the saucer should be facing you.

2 Paint the bottom and the sides of the plant saucer. Follow the directions on the paint can. You will probably need several coats of paint.

3 Let the paint dry. When it's completely dry, you can use the chalk to write on the saucer. The old sock or rag is your eraser. Now you can sit on the floor cross-legged and pretend to be a scribe. You can practice writing the alphabet or hieroglyphic symbols!

45

Supplies

8-inch terra cotta plant saucer, clean and dry

newspaper

chalkboard paint, from any paint store

brush

chalk

an old sock or rag

AMULETS, CLOTHES & MAKEUP

Ancient Egyptians cared about how they looked. They wanted clothes that looked nice. They also wanted clothes that would keep them cool in the hot, desert weather. And guess what? Their clothes did both.

Most ancient Egyptian clothing was made out of a lightweight material called **linen**. Men wore short, wraparound skirts called kilts. Women wore dresses. Long, tight–fitting dresses called sheath dresses were popular. Both men and women wore **tunics**. Tunics were kind of like long T–shirts. Young children often wore no clothes. Nudity wasn't a big deal in ancient Egypt. Most people either

went barefoot or wore simple sandals made out of papyrus. These sandals looked kind of like the flip-flops we have today.

Ancient Egyptians wore their hair in many styles. Depending on the time period, styles were short or long, curly or straight. Women often wore beautiful headbands called *diadems*. Wigs were common, too. Men and women wore them to cover their bald heads. Ancient Egyptians sometimes shaved their heads to stay cool. Until they became teenagers, boys' and girls' heads were shaved except for an "S" shaped curl on the side of their heads. This curl was called the "side-lock of youth."

JUST FOR LAUGHS

Q. What did the wig say to the head?

A. Don't worry, I've got ya covered!

Makeup was a part of ancient Egyptian fashion, too. Both men and women wore it. The most popular type of makeup was **kohl**. This was the thick, black makeup ancient Egyptians wore around their eyes. It was worn for beauty as well as health. Kohl, made from a ground up mineral called galena, helped protect the wearer's eyes from the sun's glare. It was kept in special containers called kohl pots. Women used other things from nature, like henna (a plant) and ochre (another mineral) to color their hair, nails, and lips.

47

JUST FOR LAUGHS

Knock, knock.

Who's there?

Sphinx.

Sphinx who?

Me sphinx you've forgotten me already!

AMULETS

Jewelry was very popular in ancient Egypt. Egyptians wore all kinds of gold and silver rings, bracelets, and earrings as well as beaded, collar necklaces. Some of the jewelry they wore was for decoration. But some of it was worn for another reason. These pieces of jewelry were called **amulets.** They were the lucky charms the ancient Egyptians wore or carried for protection. The Egyptians also buried these charms with the dead so that loved ones would be protected in the afterlife.

48

COMMON SYMBOLS USED AS AMULETS

Ankh: This amulet was based on the hieroglyphic symbol for life and was worn for everlasting life.

Udjat: This amulet is also called the Sacred Eye or the Eye of Horus. It was used for overall protection. It represented the eye the god Horus lost in a fight and then had magically fixed.

Scarab: This amulet was used for life after death. It represented the dung beetle. The way the dung beetle rolled a ball of dung on the ground reminded the Egyptians of the sun rolling across the sky, with each new day representing rebirth.

Djed: This amulet looks kind of like a backbone. It was worn to protect the spine.

Ancient Egyptian amulets came in all kinds of shapes. Some looked like animals such as fish or frogs. Others looked like gods or goddesses or other objects such as a heart. (Heart amulets looked like real hearts! Isn't that cool?) Each had a special power. For example, a fish-shaped amulet was used to protect someone from drowning. Sometimes ancient Egyptians wore amulets because they wanted a certain characteristic. For example, they might have worn a lion amulet so they could be as strong as a lion.

Words 2 Know

linen: lightweight fabric used to make clothes in ancient Egypt.

tunic: a piece of clothing worn by ancient Egyptian men and women.

amulet: a special charm that is worn or carried to give the owner protection.

kohl: thick, black makeup worn around the eyes.

Great Sphinx: a large, ancient Egyptian sculpture that looks like a lion with a man's head.

nemes: a head covering that pharaohs wore when they weren't wearing their crowns.

49

WOW

Ancient Egyptians wore perfume. Because they made it from beeswax or animal fat, their perfume was solid. They rubbed it on their bodies to smell good and to help protect their skin from the harsh desert climate. Ancient Egyptians used essential oils from a variety of plants to make their perfumes. Some of the common oils were cinnamon, ginger, and sandalwood. Perfumes were found in King Tut's tomb. Even after being buried for thousands of years, they still had some of their smell!

TATTOOS

Tattoos are permanent pictures or designs on the skin. Artists make them by injecting the skin with ink. Some ancient Egyptians had tattoos. We know this because we can see them in ancient Egyptian art. Some tattoos have been found on mummies, too. According to the pictures and mummies, it seems that mainly women got tattoos in ancient Egypt. Not all ancient Egyptian women had tattoos, of course. But many dancers and even Queen Nefertiti may have had them!

The ancient Egyptians didn't invent tattoos. Tattoos had been around for a long time. We don't know why ancient Egyptians had them. They might have been used to protect the wearer, like an amulet. Or maybe ancient Egyptians just liked the way they looked. Ancient Egyptian women who didn't want permanent tattoos sometimes dyed their skin with henna. Henna designs wore off the skin after a while.

COOL ARTIFACT

You've probably seen pictures of the **Great Sphinx** before. But have you ever noticed what it's wearing on its head? That special headdress is called a **nemes**. This tight-fitting, long piece of material is what pharaohs wore when they weren't wearing their crowns.

MAKE A COLLAR NECKLACE

A fancy, ancient Egyptian collar necklace is called a *wesekh*. They were originally amulets used to help protect someone in the after-life. But people liked them so much that they became a popular piece of jewelry to wear while still alive!

1 Cut the paper plate in half. Glue the two pieces together so that they make a two-layer half circle.

2 Next, cut a small, half oval in the top of the paper plate.

3 In the center of one top side, punch a hole. The hole should be about one inch from the top. Now, punch a hole in the other side.

4 Use the glue to attach the beads to the plate. You can make any kind of design you'd like! You can put the beads in straight lines or cover the whole plate. You can make a pattern with the beads or glue them on randomly.

5 When the glue is dry, put the pieces of yarn through the holes in the plate and tie them to the plate. Now, tie the collar necklace around your neck and show off your Egyptian style!

Supplies

paper plate
glue
scissors
hole punch
lots of beads
2 pieces of yarn,
10 inches long

MAKE AN EGYPTIAN

Ancient Egyptians made wigs out of animal hair or human hair. Here's an easy way to make one with yarn.

1 Cut an eight-inch circle out of the felt. An easy way to do this is to trace an 8-inch salad plate or lid of a plastic container.

2 Next, cut the yarn into pieces that are about 12 inches long. The more pieces of yarn you cut, the thicker your wig will be. If you want to jazz things up, braid the strands! This will also help make the wig thicker.

3 Cover most of the felt with a layer of glue, but leave a thin line (about one-quarter inch) down the middle of the circle free of glue. This will be your wig's part.

4 Begin attaching the strands by laying them on the piece of felt. The strands should be perpendicular to the wig's part. Half of the strands should touch the part and go to the left. The other half of the strands should touch the part and go to the right.

Supplies

one piece of black felt, 8 by 11 inches

scissors

lots of yarn

glue

WIG

5 Keep adding strands until you're happy with the wig's thickness. Cut some shorter pieces of yarn to make bangs. Let the glue dry before putting on your wig.

FRONT

THEN & NOW

THEN: Ancient Egyptian children wore tunics, dresses, or wore no clothes at all.

NOW: Today in Egypt, children wear jeans, T-shirts, and tennis shoes.

MAKE A CUFF BRACELET

The ancient Egyptians loved to wear jewelry! Since you'll be using pointy scissors and spray paint, you'll need an adult to help you with this project.

1 Use the scissors to poke a hole near the top of your canister. Cut all the way around the canister.

2 Poke another hole in the canister about 2½ inches from the first cut. Cut all the way around the canister again. You should now have a cylinder.

3 Cut a second, 2½-inch-wide cylinder from the canister.

4 Slip one of the cylinders around your wrist. If it's too big, cut the cylinder vertically. Next, overlap the cardboard until it fits. You should be able to slip the bracelet on and off easily. Glue the pieces together. Use the two paper clips to hold the pieces in place until the glue dries.

5 Measure, cut, and glue the second cylinder in the same way.

6 After the glue dries, remove the paper clips. Spread newspaper over your work area. Now, use the fabric paint to make various Egyptian designs. For example, you might want to paint an anhk, a sun, a feather, waves, or the Sacred Eye. You can use glue to make the designs, too. If you do this, be sure to turn the cylinder on its side to dry. Otherwise, the glue will run. Let the paint completely dry before moving on to the next step. This might take a couple of days.

7 Once the fabric paint has dried, follow the directions on the can to spray paint the bracelets. Be sure to paint the insides of the bracelets, too.

8 After the paint dries you can glue some plastic jewels to the outside of your bracelet, if you'd like.

55

Supplies

Pringles canister, empty and clean

scissors

glue

4 paper clips

newspaper

fabric paint, slick or puffy

gold or silver spray paint

plastic jewels (optional)

MAKE A TUNIC

With your wig and jewelry, you'll be ready for any ancient Egyptian occasion!

1 Fold your material in half widthwise. Hold it up against your body with the fold by your neck. The material should hang to your knees. Cut the length if necessary.

2 Lay the material flat on a table or on the floor. Next, cut a "T" shape out of the material. Important: the top of your "T" should be right on the fold.

3 Cut out a small half-oval at the top of the "T" for your neck hole.

4 Glue the sides of the tunic and bottom of the sleeves together. If you have a sewing machine, you can sew these seams.

5 Turn the tunic inside out so that the seams will look neat.

6 Finally, decorate the collar or the sleeve edges with fabric paint. Ancient Egyptian tunics were usually pretty plain. If you want, you can also add a sash using some craft rope or leftover material.

Supplies

2 or 2½ yards of white, lightweight material like muslin or an old sheet

scissors

fabric glue

fabric paint, various colors

56

KING TUT & OTHER COOL KINGS

Ancient Egypt was a very organized civilization. That kind of organization needs a leader. Ancient Egyptians didn't have presidents to rule the land. They had kings called **pharaohs**.

Ancient Egyptians believed their kings were living gods. Because of this, kings had absolute power. This means they had complete control over everything in ancient Egypt. In other words, what they said went! Kings were not elected. The job was usually handed down from father to son. There were some female rulers, though. One was Queen Hatshepsut. She was a great ruler who boldly took the throne from her young stepson and ruled from 1473 to 1458 BCE. Another female ruler was Cleopatra. She was a beautiful and smart queen and ancient Egypt's last pharaoh. She ruled from 51 to 30 BCE.

COOL ARTIFACT

Artists often showed ancient Egyptians holding a **crook** and a **flail**. They were symbols of the king's power. Most kings were buried holding a crook and flail across their chests.

Kings and their families lived in beautiful homes. They had lots of riches such as jewels and gold. They also had many servants. Like other kings, ancient Egyptian kings wore crowns. There were many different kinds of crowns. There are three that most people recognize though. One is the red crown. This crown looked sort of like a chair leaning backwards. It was the crown the ruler of Lower Egypt wore. The second crown, worn by the ruler of Upper Egypt, was the white crown. It looked kind of like a bowling pin! The third crown was the double crown. It was a combination of the red and white crowns. The kings who ruled after Lower and Upper Egypt were united wore this crown.

58

WOW

Pharaohs had all the power in ancient Egypt. If you imagine the way ancient Egypt was organized as a pyramid, you could say kings were at the top.

PYRAMID OF POWER

- PHARAOHS
- ROYAL FAMILY
- HIGH PRIESTS, ADVISORS
- GOVENORS, TAX COLLECTORS
- SCRIBES
- SKILLED CRAFTSMEN
- FARMERS, PEASANTS
- SLAVES

THE BOY KING

You probably know King Tutankhamen by another name: King Tut! King Tut ruled from 1336 to 1327 BCE. He was just nine years old when he became king. This is why he is nicknamed the Boy King. He wasn't an especially great king. And he died around age 19. So why is he one of the most famous of all ancient Egyptian kings? It's because of his tomb.

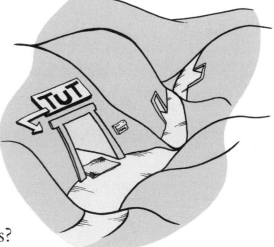

In order to keep the kings' tombs safe from grave robbers, the ancient Egyptians began burying their dead in a secret place. This happened around 1550 to 1069 BCE. This secret place is called the **Valley of the Kings**. King Tut was one of the kings buried there. But, unlike a lot of other tombs, King Tut's tomb wasn't found until 1922. It was found by archaeologist Howard Carter and his business partner Lord Carnarvon. After being robbed in ancient times, it had been sealed and hidden for thousands of years! King Tut's tomb held so many treasures that it took over 10 years to remove and clean them all. The treasure included things like solid gold sandals and ivory Senet game boards.

59

WONDERFUL THINGS

This is how Howard Carter described finding King Tut's treasure:

"At first I could see nothing, but as my eyes grew accustomed to the light, details of the room within emerged slowly. Strange animals, statues and gold—everywhere the glint of gold. For a moment…I was struck dumb with amazement, and when Lord Carnarvon, unable to stand the suspense any longer, inquired anxiously, 'Can you see anything?' it was all I could do to get out the words, 'Yes, wonderful things!'"

Today, King Tut's treasure travels to museums all over the world. King Tut's mummy is still in the Valley of the Kings.

WAS KING TUT'S TOMB CURSED?

Do you believe in curses? Legend has it that King Tut's tomb had a curse. This warning said, "Death shall come on swift wings to him who disturbs the peace of the king."

Many people believed the curse was true. They believed King Tut looked for revenge on anyone who broke into his tomb. This was probably because a few strange things happened. First of all, Lord Carnarvon (one of the people who helped find the tomb) became ill and died after being bitten by a mosquito. This happened just six months after King Tut's tomb was opened. Second, other people who helped find King Tut's tomb became ill, too. None of these other people died untimely deaths, though. And Howard Carter, who actually opened the door, lived for another 17 years. Other strange things supposedly happened as well. One rumor was that a cobra—a symbol of the pharaohs—ate Howard Carter's pet bird.

Many modern scientists believe that a bacteria or mold made tomb visitors sick. People like mysterious things, though. And so the idea that King Tut's tomb was cursed lives on!

60

pharaoh: another name for ancient Egyptian kings or rulers.

Valley of the Kings: a remote valley where the ancient Egyptians began burying their kings around 1550 to 1069 BCE to keep their tombs safe from grave robbers.

crook: an item carried by ancient Egyptian king. It looked like a short cane or shepherd's staff.

flail: Another item carried by ancient Egyptian kings. This short rod had three beaded strands attached to the top.

DIGGING DEEPER INTO FAMOUS PHARAOHS

You've already read about Queen Hatshepsut, Queen Cleopatra, and King Tut. Here are some other ancient Egyptian rulers who are famous.

Khufu: Khufu built the Great Pyramid. This pyramid is near the modern capital of Cairo. It is the largest pyramid in the world. When it was built, it was over 480 feet tall. Its base takes up about 13 acres of land! Khufu ruled from 2589 to 2566 BCE.

Akhenaton: Akhenaton was married to Queen Nefertiti and might be King Tut's father. Akhenaton made the ancient Egyptians mad because he wanted them to worship just one god instead of lots of gods. He ruled from 1352 to 1336 BCE.

Rameses II: Rameses II was also known as Rameses the Great. He ruled a very long time, from 1279 to 1213. That's 66 years! He built more monuments and temples than any other king. Rameses' mummy is one of the best-preserved mummies ever found.

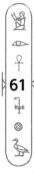

61

THEN & NOW

THEN: Kings ruled ancient Egypt.

NOW: An elected president and a prime minister run Egypt together.

MAKE A FALSE BEARD

Ancient Egyptian kings didn't have facial hair. The long beards you see on statues or in art are fake beards. These beards were tied on. They were usually blue, but we don't know why.

1 Use your finger or a paint brush to spread a thin layer of glue on the outside of the toilet paper roll.

2 Start at one end of the roll and wrap the yarn around and around the roll. You want to make sure the lines of yarn are right next to each other. It's kind of like you're winding a spool of thread. When you reach the end, cut the yarn and tuck the end inside the roll with a bit of glue. Let the glue dry.

3 After the glue is dry, ask an adult to poke two holes, one on each side of the top of the roll.

4 Make a knot in one end of a pipe cleaner by twisting the end. Thread the other end of the pipe cleaner through the hole from the inside. Pull the end of the pipe cleaner until the knot is resting against the hole on the inside.

5 Attach the second pipe cleaner in the second hole the same way.

6 Hold the false beard next to your chin. Attach it to your face by wrapping the pipe cleaners around your ears. Now, you're ready to rock-n-rule!

Supplies

1 empty toilet paper roll

glue

paintbrush

blue yarn

scissors or hole punch

2 pipe cleaners

MAKE KING TUT SANDALS

You'll be using spray paint for this project so keep an adult handy.

1 Lay newspaper over your work area. Since you're going to be painting, make sure the area has plenty of ventilation.

2 Follow the directions on the paint can to spray paint the tops, sides, and bottoms of the flip-flops. Let them dry. Note that you'll have to paint the tops and sides and let them dry before painting the bottoms.

3 Decorate your sandals. Glue plastic jewels and sequins and glitter to them. If you want, you can use permanent markers to draw hieroglyphic symbols on the sandals. You can leave them plain gold, too, if you like.

4 Let the glue dry. Now, you're ready to go walking in high Egyptian style!

Supplies

newspaper

an old or inexpensive pair of flip-flops

small can of spray paint

glue

plastic jewels, sequins, and glitter

permanent markers (optional)

PLAY "WHO'S

Ancient Egyptian kings had absolute power. People had to do whatever they said! In this game, players take turns finding out what it's like to be completely in charge of a group.

To play

1 Everyone sits or stands in a circle. One person is sent away to another room or another part of the yard to cover their eyes. This person will be the guesser.

2 While the guesser is away, the rest of the group picks a king. If there's a grownup around, he or she can pick someone to be the king.

3 Once a king is picked, he or she should start leading the group in an action. For example, the king and group could hop, make silly faces, rub their stomachs, skip, snap or clap, tap their chins, or run in place. Use your imagination!

THE KING?"

4 Invite the guesser back to the circle. While the guesser watches the group, the king should keep changing actions. Whatever the king does, the rest of the group should follow BUT they should try to do it without giving the identity of the king away! One good way to keep the king's identity hidden is to watch him or her out of the corner of their eyes. They can also just watch the person across from them in the circle.

JUST FOR LAUGHS

Q: Which pharaoh played a musical instrument?

A: King Toot.

----

5 While the group secretly imitates the king, the guesser tries to guess who is leading the group.

6 The guesser gets three chances to guess who is king. If he or she correctly guesses the identity of the king, the person who was king now becomes the guesser. The first guesser rejoins the group and gets to pick the next king.

7 If the guesser can't guess the king's identity after three attempts, he or she has to go cover his or her eyes and be the guesser again. The group then needs to pick a new king. If the guesser can't guess the king's identity a second time, he or she returns to the group and the second king becomes the new guesser.

65

Supplies

a bunch of friends (the more the better!)

a large area to move around in

PLAY

"VALLEY OF THE KINGS"

In this game, you and your friends hunt for hidden treasure. You can pretend you are part of Howard Carter's team searching for King Tut's long-lost tomb! You can play the game indoors or outdoors. You should have one less rock than you do players.

To Play

1 Wrap each rock in a piece of foil. These will be your pieces of treasure. Each player—except one—should have a piece of treasure. The person without any treasure is the hider.

2 Choose a place to be your "temple." It can be a couch, a porch step, a rug, a corner—wherever you like!

3 The players stay at the temple. The hider collects all the treasure from the players and hides each piece in a different place in another room or area of the yard. The other players should close their eyes so they can't see the hider hiding the treasure. No peeking!

4 After all of the treasure is hidden, the players leave the temple and go searching for it. After a player finds a piece of treasure, he or she should pick it up and return to the temple.

5 The last person to find a piece of treasure and return to the temple becomes the new hider.

6 There are no winners or losers in this game. Just keep taking turns hiding and finding the treasure until everyone decides to end the game!

Supplies

small rocks (not pebbles)

aluminum foil

3 to 6 friends (you can play with more people, but you'll need more rocks.)

MUMMIES & PYRAMIDS

When you think of ancient Egypt, what usually pops into your mind? It's probably what pops into other people's minds: **mummies**, **pyramids**, **temples**, and **hieroglyphs**! These are some of the most interesting things about ancient Egypt. They teach us a lot about the people who lived so long ago.

MUMMIES

Mummies might seem kind of creepy looking, but the ancient Egyptians didn't make them to scare people. Ancient Egyptians believed people needed their bodies in the afterlife. To stop the decay of bodies, they used a process called **mummification.** Mummies are bodies that have gone through this process.

When a person died in ancient Egypt, their body was taken to someone called an **embalmer**. It was the embalmer's job to mummify a body. Making a mummy took 70 days! First, the body was washed. Then all the organs, except for the heart, were removed and put into special jars called **canopic jars**. The organs of a body are things like the liver and lungs. The heart was left in the body because ancient Egyptians believed it was the most important organ.

Then the embalmer dried out the body using a kind of salt called **natron**. When the body was dried out it was filled with sawdust or

68

BOOK OF THE DEAD

Embalmers placed a special book inside the coffins of each mummy. The *Book of the Dead* was a collection of spells and instructions for making the journey into the afterlife. For example, here is the spell that the person who died was supposed to use when it came time for his or her heart to be judged by Osiris, the god of the underworld:

"O my heart . . . do not stand up as a witness against me in the judgment hall . . . do not tell them what I have really done!"

We have many copies of the *Book of the Dead* to study. This is because there were so many of them made. And luckily for us, many of them survived over time. Sometimes, rich ancient Egyptians had the name and picture of the person who died added to a copy!

Words 2 Know

mummy: a body that has gone through the mummification process.

pyramid: large, stone structures with square bases and triangular sides where pharaohs were buried.

hieroglyphs: the symbols that made up ancient Egyptian writing.

mummification: a process where a dead body is kept from decaying.

embalmer: a person whose job it was to mummify a body.

canopic jars: special jars where the organs of a dead person were kept after they were removed during mummification.

natron: a kind of salt that was used to dry out a body during mummification.

sarcophagus: a large, stone box where coffins were placed.

straw and spices and covered in melted resin, a kind of natural plastic. Finally, the embalmer wrapped the body in strips of linen. Each finger and toe was wrapped, and then the whole body was wrapped. After the wrapping, embalmers put the mummy inside a coffin. Then, they put the coffin inside a big, stone box called a **sarcophagus.** At last, everything was put into a tomb. Common folks were buried in cemeteries. But kings and their families were buried in a special place.

BOOK of the DEAD

WHAT HAPPENED TO ALL THE MUMMIES?

Even though we have many copies of the *Book of the Dead* to study, we don't have lots and lots of mummies to study. There are two reasons for this. One, people throughout history have collected mummies. Mummies are pretty interesting! Many of these mummies have been lost or broken. And two, mummies were once a popular ingredient in medicines. People calling themselves doctors ground them up and mixed them into potions. These potions were supposed to cure all kinds of ills, but they often just made people sicker!

PYRAMIDS

Because they were considered living gods, ancient Egyptian kings had their coffins buried in a special place. These special places were pyramids. Pyramids are very large, stone structures with square bases and triangular sides. There are about 100 ancient Egyptian pyramids still standing.

Ancient Egyptians didn't build true pyramids right away. It took hundreds of years for them to get it right. Some early pyramids looked like steps. Others had sides that curved. Eventually, they got it right. And sometime between 2589 and 2566 BCE King Khufu had the **Great Pyramid** built. This pyramid is the biggest one in the world. It has over two million stones and is about 450 feet tall and 745 feet long. It took over 20 years to build!

No one knows for sure how the ancient Egyptians built the pyramids. They did not leave any directions. Most experts think the builders moved the large, heavy stones with sledges.

A sledge is a simple machine that uses logs and a board to roll objects. Most experts now believe skilled workers built the pyramids. In the past, some people thought slaves built the pyramids. It probably took between 20,000 and 30,000 workers to build a pyramid. There is evidence that these workers lived in villages made just for them near the building site. Egyptologists have found houses and shops and bakeries! Besides workers' houses, there were other buildings near pyramids. Some of these buildings were temples.

THE GREAT SPHINX

Many photographs of the pyramids show an interesting statue in the front or nearby. This famous statue looks like a crouching lion with a man's head. The head is that of King Khafra. This king was the son of King Khufu, the pharaoh who built the Great Pyramid. This statue is called the Great Sphinx. It is about 240 feet long and 60 feet tall. It was carved out of limestone. Long ago, it was painted and even had a beard! Now, the paint has worn off and the beard is gone.

Besides its beard, the Great Sphinx is missing part of his nose. No one is really sure what happened to it. One of the most popular myths is that it was blown away during target practice by soldiers in the late 1700s. This is not true, but people still tell the story. All we do know for sure is there are marks near the nose that suggest tools were used to remove it.

HOW DID THEY CUT THOSE BIG PYRAMID STONES?

There are over 2 million stones in the Great Pyramid. Each of these stones weighs thousands of pounds! Ancient Egyptians didn't have jackhammers or big bulldozers to cut the stones. So how did they do it? Sometimes they used simple hand tools like chisels. That must have been very hard work! Other times, they used water. Yep. You read that correctly. They used water. First they would cut a small hole in the stone. Next, they would jam a piece of wood into the hole. After this, they poured water onto the wood. The water made the wood expand. When this happened, the wood pushed on the stone and broke it.

TEMPLES

Ancient Egyptians believed gods could live inside statues. These statues needed houses. So ancient Egyptians built temples.

Early temples were pretty small. But later on in history, ancient Egyptians built huge, fancy temples. Some of these temples had stone columns that were nearly 70 feet tall! Temples weren't places where ordinary people could visit, though. The only ones allowed inside a temple were **priests** and pharaohs. Ancient Egyptian priests weren't really religious leaders, though. It was the priests' job to take care of the god statue and the temple.

Temples weren't built just to honor gods. Some temples were built in honor of pharaohs who were still alive. For example, Rameses the Great had a temple built. Queen Hatshepsut also had a temple built so she could write down all the things she did as pharaoh.

PRIESTS

When we think of a priest, we usually think of someone who is a religious leader. We think of someone who preaches or leads us in worship. In ancient Egypt, being a priest was just a job, but it was a pretty good job! Many priests came from rich families. The pharaoh usually appointed priests, or the job was handed down from father to son. Priests were respected. The Egyptian title for priest was *hem netjer*. It meant "servant of the god."

It was the high priest's job to take care of the statue of the god. They washed and dressed the statues and left food and drink. The priests were also responsible for carrying the god statue during festivals. Festivals were yearly celebrations when everyone came out to honor a god. During

73

JUST FOR LAUGHS

Q • Who was the best mummy wrapper in ancient Egypt?

A: The Wizard of Gauze!

COOL ARTIFACT

Obelisks are tall, skinny, stone monuments with pointed tops. Ancient Egyptians often placed two of them in front of temples. We're not sure why. Some experts think it had to do with worshiping the sun.

these festivals, priests carried the heavy statues through the streets on special carriers shaped liked boats. These carriers were called bark shrines.

The high priest also opened the shrine every day. A **shrine** is a special cabinet where the god statue was kept. Other priests were in charge of taking care of the temple. They did the cleaning and the gardening and handled record keeping.

Priests worked in shifts. This means they took turns working throughout the year. A priest's shift normally lasted a month. While they weren't on duty, priests lived with their families and went to their other jobs. When they were on duty, though, priests had lots of rules to follow. For example, they were expected to shave the hair off their bodies and bathe several times a day. This was to show they were pure and clean.

HIEROGLYPHS

Along with mummies, pyramids, and temples, ancient Egyptians are known for their written symbols. This writing is called hieroglyphs. It is made up of hundreds of symbols. Some of these symbols represented sounds. Other symbols represented whole words. And still other symbols gave readers information such as whether a name belonged to a woman or a man.

74

THEN & NOW

THEN: Ancient Egyptians spoke Egyptian and used hieroglyphs to write things down.

NOW: The official language of Egypt is Arabic.

WOW

Would you like to write your name using the hieroglyphic alphabet? Use this chart to help you.

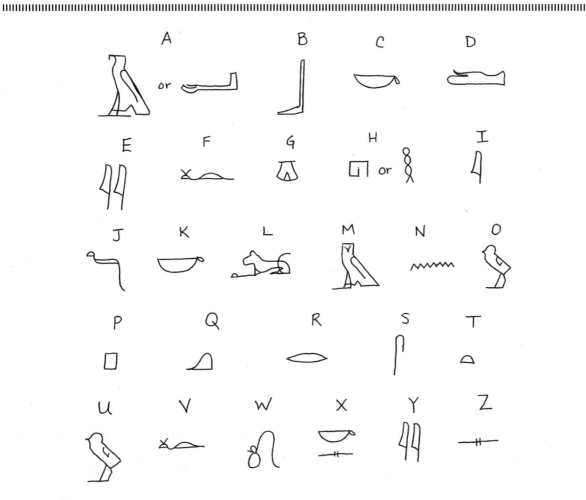

75

The ancient Egyptians used pictures or symbols to show numbers too. For the numbers 1 through 9, they just used strokes or lines. For number 4, they drew four strokes or lines. For the number 10, they drew a picture of a cattle hobble. This symbol looked like an upside down "U." A picture of a coiled rope represented the number 100. The symbol for 1,000 was a lotus plant. A picture of a frog represented 100,000. And a picture of a god with raised arms was used to show the number 1,000,000.

In our math system, we use place values. This means the order of the numbers is important because it tells us how many hundreds, tens, or ones we have in a numeral. The ancient Egyptian's math system was different. There were no place values. Because each symbol represented a number, all numbers were just grouped together. They were usually written from largest to smallest, though. For example, to write 1001, the Egyptians would have drawn one lotus plant and one stroke.

It was a scribe's job to read and write hieroglyphs. Reading and writing hieroglyphs wasn't easy. It could take 10 years to learn them all. How did Egyptologists learn to read hieroglyphs? Believe it or not, a stone taught them! The Rosetta Stone is a stone with the same information written in three different languages. One of those languages is hieroglyphs. Another is Greek. A French man named Jean-François Champollion studied the writing on the stone and was able to translate it. This happened in 1822. Ever since then, Egyptologists have been using hieroglyphs to learn more about ancient Egypt.

Words 2 Know

Great Pyramid: the largest pyramid in the world; it was built by King Khufu.

priest: an ancient Egyptian man whose job it was to take care of the temple and god statue.

shrine: a special box or cabinet where ancient Egyptians kept statues of gods.

JUST FOR LAUGHS

- Why don't mummies take vacations?
- They are afraid to relax and unwind.

MAKE A HIEROGLYPH TABLET

Ancient Egyptian scribes would use a brush and ink to write hieroglyphs. But they also chiseled hieroglyphs into stone. Here's a fun way to get the same look. You'll be using spray paint for this project, so ask an adult to help.

1 Spread the clay evenly to cover the surface of the foam board. Smooth the surface with your fingers.

2 Open your paper clip so you can use it like a pencil. You need a fine, sharp tip. Pointy scissors work okay, but pens and pencils don't work as well as a paper clip.

3 Use the paper clip to etch hieroglyphs into the clay. You can use pictures and symbols to tell a story about your days as a pharaoh! Or maybe you can make your own Rosetta Stone. You can erase a mistake by smoothing over your marks with your fingers.

4 After you're done etching, spread the newspaper out. Follow the directions on the spray paint can to paint the foam board. You will need only one coat of paint. Step back and admire your own hieroglyph tablet!

Supplies
foam board
air-hardening clay
1 paper clip
newspaper
1 small can of light brown spray paint

You'll be working with food for this activity. Make sure you wash your hands before you begin.

1 Off to one side of your work space, lay down a sheet of wax paper. Sprinkle it with a bit of flour.

2 In the bowl, mix together the peanut butter, powdered milk, powdered sugar, and honey.

3 After you've mixed the ingredients together, take the dough out of the bowl and place it on the wax paper. Knead the dough until it's smooth.

4 Pinch off 4 sections of dough and roll them into balls. Using dough in the corners, make a pretzel rod square.

5 Use the remaining pretzel rods and another ball of dough to make a pyramid shape.

78

Supplies

wax paper
flour
medium-size mixing bowl
½ cup peanut butter
1 cup powdered milk
1 cup powdered sugar
¾ cup honey
spoon
8 long pretzel rods

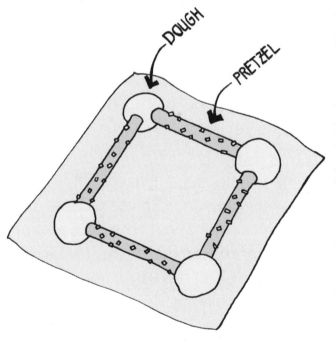

DOUGH

PRETZEL

EDIBLE PYRAMID

6 You can eat your pyramid right away or wait until you show it off! If you want to save it for later or if you have extra dough, store these things in an airtight container in the refrigerator. Yum!

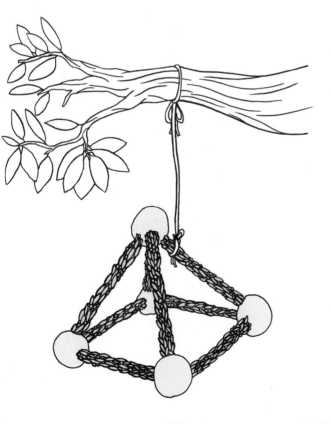

Variation:
Pyramid Bird Feeder

You can make an edible pyramid to share with your feathered friends. Coat the pretzel rods with peanut butter and roll them in birdseed before you put the pyramid together. Next, tie a piece of yarn around the top of the pyramid and hang your feeder from a tree branch.

MAKE A

A *sistrum* was a rattle-like musical instrument. Women priests and royal wives and daughters used them during ceremonies such as funerals. Have a grownup help you with the hammer and nail.

1 Starting at one end of the cardboard, wrap masking tape around and around until you've covered the entire length of the cardboard.

2 Fold the cardboard in half. Don't crease the top. Holding the two ends together, wrap masking tape around the bottom 5 inches to make a handle.

3 Open up the top 7 inches so it looks like a skinny tennis racket.

4 Using the hammer and nail, poke holes through both layers of cardboard. Make one set of holes an inch from the top, another set of holes 2 inches from the top, and the third set 3 inches from the top.

5 Straighten out the paper clips. Carefully poke a paper clip through the top hole on one side of the hoop.

Supplies

piece of cardboard that is 1½ inches wide and 24 inches long

masking tape

hammer and nail

3 paper clips

15 small, metal washers

permanent markers, various colors

SISTRUM

6 Thread five of the washers onto the paper clip wire in the space between the pieces of cardboard. Carefully poke the paper clip through the hole on the other side of the cardboard.

7 Fold over about ¼ to ½ inch of the wire on each end so the paper clip can't pull out of the cardboard. Tape the folded wire to the outside of the hoop with the masking tape.

8 Add the next paper clip and five washers the same way through the next set of holes.

9 Add the last paper clip and the rest of the washers through the final pair of holes.

10 Decorate your sistrum using permanent markers. You're ready to make some noise!

EXPLORE

Ancient Egyptians learned about mummification by trying different kinds of things. In this activity, you can observe which ingredients preserve an apple best. One of the ingredients is ice. Of course, the ancient Egyptians didn't have ice. But animals and people have been found frozen in ice. This is a natural kind of mummification. You'll be using a knife, so ask an adult to help with this activity.

1 Wash and dry the apple. Cut it into four slices.

2 Fill one of the cups with water. The water should completely cover the apple slice but be about ½ to 1 inch from the top of the cup. Put this cup in the freezer. Make sure it's in a place where it won't get knocked over.

3 Put the other three slices in each of the rest of the cups.

4 Wrap one of the slices in the gauze. Make sure you wrap the gauze tightly around the whole apple slice. Put the slice in one of the cups.

5 In the mixing bowl, combine the baking soda and salt.

6 Pour the baking soda and salt mixture on top of another of the apple slices. Make sure no part of the apple slice is showing.

Supplies

1 small apple

knife

1 yard of medical gauze

4 plastic cups

½ cup baking soda

½ cup salt

small mixing bowl

spoon

water

freezer

MUMMIFICATION

7 Don't do anything to the last apple slice.

8 Place these three plastic cups in a dark, dry place for one week. No peeking!

9 After a week, take all the apple slices out. Let the ice melt off the first apple slice. Unwrap the second apple slice. And carefully dust the baking soda and salt off the third apple slice. Don't rinse this slice. The fourth slice is ready to go.

Important: Don't eat any of the apple slices!

Things to think about

👁 Which apple slice has decayed or rotted the least?

👁 Which apple slice has decayed or rotted the most?

👁 What does the apple slice that's been in the baking soda and salt look like? Does it look kind of like a mummy? In what way?

👁 Why do you think the apple slice that's been in the ice hasn't decayed?

👁 What do you think causes decay?

GLOSSARY

afterlife: the ancient Egyptians believed in life after death.

amulet: a special charm that is worn or carried to give the owner protection.

apprentice: someone who learns to do a job by working for someone who already does the job.

archaeologist: someone who studies ancient cultures by looking at artifacts.

artifact: a simple object like a tool or piece of pottery from a culture or time period.

bartering: a system where people trade one thing for another.

BCE: an abbreviation that means Before Common Era.

Bes: the ancient Egyptian household god of fun and games.

canopic jars: special jars where the organs of a dead person were kept after being removed during mummification.

CE: an abbreviation that means Common Era, after the birth of Christ.

clay: a material found in nature that is sticky and easily molded when wet and hard when baked or dried.

crook: an item carried by ancient Egyptian kings; it looked like a short cane or shepherd's staff.

Egyptologist: someone who studies ancient Egypt.

84

embalmer: a person whose job it was to mummify a body.

ferment: a chemical breaking down of a substance caused by an enzyme.

flail: an item carried by ancient Egyptian kings; it was a short rod that had three beaded strands attached to the top.

god: a being believed to have special, superhuman powers.

goddess: a female god.

Great Pyramid: the largest pyramid in the world; it was built by King Khufu.

Great Sphinx: a large, ancient Egyptian sculpture that looks like a lion with a man's head.

harvest: to pick or pull crops out of the ground when they are ripe.

hieroglyphs: the symbols that made up ancient Egyptian writing.

inundation: another word for flooding.

kohl: thick, black makeup worn aroud the eyes.

linen: lightweight fabric used to make clothes in ancient Egypt.

lyrics: words to songs.

mash: grain soaked in hot water to be used in making alcohol.

mudbricks: bricks made using clay, pebbles, straw, and water and dried in the sun.

mummification: a process where a dead body is kept from decaying.

mummy: a body that has gone through the mummification process.

natron: a kind of salt that was used to dry out a body during mummification.

nemes: a head covering that pharaohs wore when they weren't wearing their crowns.

Nile River: the longest river in the world and an important part of life in ancient Egypt.

ostraca: a piece of pottery used to practice writing.

papyriform boats: wooden boats that curved up at the ends to look like reed boats, often used as funeral boats.

papyrus: paper made from the papyrus plant and used by the ancient Egyptians.

pharaoh: another name for ancient Egyptian kings or rulers.

priest: a person who helped take care of sick people and took care of and ran the temples in ancient Egypt.

pyramid: large, stone structures with square bases and triangular sides where pharaohs were buried.

Royal Library of Alexandria: a great library in Alexandria, Egypt, that had half a million books and scrolls.

Royal Ship of Khufu: a famous example of a papyriform boat, found in pieces, buried near the Great Pyramid.

Sahara Desert: the largest and hottest desert in the world.

sarcophagus: a large, stone box where coffins were placed.

scribe: a person who read and wrote hieroglyphs, the ancient Egyptian writing.

scroll: pieces of papyrus glued together and then rolled up.

shaduf: a simple device that uses a bucket and a counterweight on a long pole to lift water out of one place and move it to another.

shrine: a special box or cabinet where ancient Egyptians kept statues of gods.

silt: the good farming soil left over after the Nile flooded.

spell: a word or group of words that the ancient Egyptians believed had magical powers to heal.

Taweret: the ancient Egyptian household goddess who protected mothers and children.

tunic: a piece of clothing worn by ancient Egyptian men and women.

Valley of the Kings: a remote valley where the ancient Egyptians began burying their kings around 1550 to 1069 BCE to keep their tombs safe from grave robbers.

RESOURCES

Books

Hart, George (consulting editor). *Discoveries: Ancient Egypt.* San Francisco: Fog City Press, 2003.

Mertz, Barbara. *Red Land, Black Land: Daily Life in Ancient Egypt.* New York: Dodd, Mead & Company, revised 1978.

Mertz, Barbara. *Temples, Tombs and Hieroglyphs: A Popular History of Ancient Egypt.* New York: Dodd, Mead & Company, revised 1978.

Pemberton, Delia. *The Atlas of Ancient Egypt.* New York: Harry N. Abrams Inc. 2005.

Ryan, Donald P. *The Complete Idiot's Guide to Ancient Egypt.* Indianapolis: Alpha Books, 2002.

Shaw, Ian, and Paul Nicholson. *The Dictionary of Ancient Egypt.* New York: Harry N. Abrams Inc., updated 2003.

Van Vleet, Carmella. *Great Ancient Egypt Projects You Can Build Yourself.* White River Junction, Vermont: Nomad Press, 2006.

Want to read more? Try these books!

Ancient Egypt: Curious Kids Guides, Philip Steele (Kingfisher, 2002)

Ancient Egypt: DK Pockets (DK Publishing, 2003)

Ancient Egypt: Modern Rhymes About Ancient Times, Susan Altman (Children's Press, 2002).

Great Ancient Egypt Projects You Can Build Yourself, Carmella Van Vleet (Nomad Press, 2006).

If I Were a Kid in Ancient Egypt (Cobblestone Publishing, 2007).

Mummies Made in Egypt, Avi (HarperTrophy, 1985).

Mummies, Pyramids and Pharaohs: A Book About Ancient Egypt, Gail Gibbons (Little Brown Young Readers, 2004)

The 5,000-year-old Puzzle: Solving a Mystery of Ancient Egypt, Claudia Logan (Farrar, Strauss & Giroux, 2002).

The Magic School Bus Ms. Frizzle's Adventures: Ancient Egypt, Joanna Cole. (Scholastic Press Inc., 2001).

You Wouldn't Want to be a Pyramid Builder, Jacqueline Morley (Franklin Watts, 2004).

Cool Websites to Check Out

A to Z Kidstuff
http://www.atozkidsstuff.com/egypt.html

Animal Mummies
http://www.animalmummies.com/

British Museum – Ancient Egypt
http://www.ancientegypt.co.uk/

CMA Kids: Egyptomania
http://www.clevelandart.org/kids/egypt/index.html

Cybersleuth Kids: Ancient Civilizations
http://cybersleuth-kids.com/sleuth/History/Ancient_Civilizations/Egypt/index.htm

History for Kids – Ancient Egypt
http://www.historyforkids.org/learn/egypt/index.htm

Pyramids: The Inside Story
http://www.pbs.org/wgbh/nova/pyramid/

The Mystery of King Tut
http://www.nationalgeographic.com/ngkids/0508/

Cool Museums to Visit

Brooklyn Museum of Art (Brooklyn, New York)
Carnegie Museum of Natural History (Pittsburg, Pennsylvania)
Cincinnati Art Museum (Cincinnati, Ohio)
Field Museum of Natural History (Chicago, Illinois)
Los Angeles County Museum of Art (Los Angles, California)
Michael C. Carlos Museum (Atlanta, Georgia)
Museum of Fine Arts (Boston, Massachusetts)
Nelson-Atkins Museum of Art (Kansas City, Missouri)
Rosicrucian Egyptian and Oriental Museum (San Jose, California)
The Cleveland Museum of Art (Cleveland, Ohio)
The Detroit Institute of Arts (Detroit, Michigan)
The Metropolitan Museum of Art (New York, New York)
University of Pennsylvania Museum (Philadelphia, Pennsylvania)
Virginia Museum of Fine Arts (Richmond, Virginia)

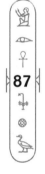

87

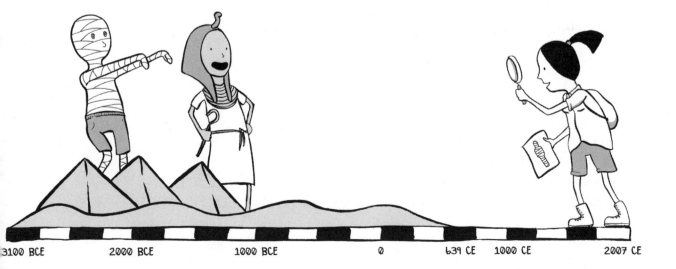

3100 BCE   2000 BCE   1000 BCE   0   639 CE   1000 CE   2007 CE

INDEX

89